# Comprehension

## Pupil Book Year 1

Shelley Welsh

# Features of this book

- Extracts from a rich variety of fiction and non-fiction texts.

- Questions split into three sections that become progressively more challenging:

- 'How did you do?' checks at the end of each topic for self-evaluation.

- Regular progress tests to assess pupils' understanding and recap on their learning.

- Answers to every question in a pull-out section at the centre of the book.

# Contents

| | |
|---|---|
| Symbols, signs and labels | 4 |
| Posters | 6 |
| Adverts | 8 |
| Information texts | 10 |
| Contents pages, glossaries and indexes | 12 |
| Instructions | 14 |
| *Progress test 1* | 16 |
| | |
| Book covers | 18 |
| Stories 1 | 20 |
| Play scripts | 22 |
| Stories 2 | 24 |
| *Progress test 2* | 26 |
| | |
| Poetry 1 | 28 |
| Poetry 2 | 30 |
| Traditional tales 1 | 32 |
| Traditional tales 2 | 34 |
| Traditional tales 3 | 36 |
| Traditional tales 4 | 38 |
| *Progress test 3* | 40 |
| | |
| *Answers (centre pull-out)* | 1–4 |

# Symbols, signs and labels

We can see symbols, signs and labels everywhere we look: your house number, the street sign where you live, the sign showing the name of your school. There are labels on your school uniform, your books and areas in your classroom. Labels can tell you who owns something, or what or where something is. If we didn't label our envelopes with a name and address, the postman wouldn't know where to go!

## Warm up

1. Look at the picture below. Grace has helped her teacher label the classroom. Can you spot what has gone wrong? Write the correct word or words on each label in the picture.

## Test yourself

② Look at the pictures below. Use the words **farm**, **airport** and **toilets** to label the pictures. Write the answer below each sign.

a) _____ b) _____ c) _____

## Challenge yourself

③ What are the birds drinking out of?

_____

④ What is the rabbit next to?

_____

⑤ Where could you sit for a rest?

_____

## How did you do?

# Posters

Posters are one way of advertising an event or a place. There isn't very much writing on a poster, and there is usually a bold image to grab your attention.

**Spring Sing**

Where: Honley Hall

When: 8th March

Time: 6:00pm

Ticket price: £2

Starring:
The Cheeky Chimps
and
The Silver Stars

## Warm up

1. Where is the event taking place? Circle **one** answer.

   **Honley Hall**
   **Hamley Hall**
   **Homely Hall**

2. When is the event taking place? Circle **one** answer.

   **6th June**
   **8th March**
   **8th May**

3. What time does the event start?

   _____

## Test yourself

4. What is being advertised in the poster? Circle **one** answer.

   **a circus**     **a concert**     **a play**     **a pantomime**

5. How much would it cost altogether if you and a friend went to the concert?

   _____

**Sam Smart's Circus**

Goose Green Park
3rd, 4th and 5th May

Two shows a day!

Afternoon: 1pm, Evening: 5pm

Adults £4, Children £2

★ Amazing Acrobats!
★ Terrific Trapeze Artists!
★ Crazy Clowns!

## Challenge yourself

6. How many days will the circus be on for?

   _____

7. How much will it cost for one adult and one child?

   _____

8. What is the name of the punctuation mark that comes after 'acrobats', 'artists' and 'clowns'? Circle **one** answer.

   **question mark**
   **exclamation mark**
   **full stop**

9. Which performers might make you laugh?

   _____

# Adverts

We see and hear adverts almost every day – on the television, in magazines, in newspapers, on the radio, in shop windows. Adverts try to persuade us to buy something.

## Warm up

**1** Tick the **two** statements below that are true.

Doctor Spock Space Boots come in one colour. ☐

Doctor Spock Space Boots come in all sizes. ☐

Doctor Spock Space Boots come in all colours. ☐

Doctor Spock Space Boots come in one size. ☐

## Test yourself

**2** What time of year would be best to wear Doctor Spock Space Boots?

_____

**3** How long has Doctor Spock been making space boots for?

_____

## Challenge yourself

**4** Who are Doctor Spock Space Boots for? Circle **one** answer.

**adults**    **grandparents**    **children**    **babies**

**5** What is your favourite thing about Doctor Spock Space boots?

_____

**6** How much would you pay for two pairs of Doctor Spock Space Boots?

_____

## How did you do?

# Information texts

In Europe, there are four seasons: spring, summer, autumn and winter.

In spring:

- the weather gets warmer
- we start to plant seeds
- chicks hatch and lambs are born
- buds start to form on plants and trees.

## Warm up

1. What is Mum doing? Circle **one** answer.

    **cutting the grass**     **planting seeds**     **playing with a ball**

2. What is Dad doing? Circle **one** answer.

    **planting seeds**     **cutting the hedge**     **playing with the dog**

3. What are the children playing with?

    _____

4. What starts to form on plants and trees in spring?

    _____

## Summer

In summer:
- the weather can be quite hot
- there is less rain which can lead to a drought (not enough water)
- it gets dark later in the evening and light earlier in the morning.

### Test yourself

5. What colour is Mum's t-shirt? _____

6. Complete the sentence below.

   The _____ is chasing the _____.

7. What is there to eat? _____

### Challenge yourself

8. What is a **drought**?
   _____

9. Why might it feel like you are going to bed in the daytime in the summer months? Circle **one** answer.

   **the weather is hotter**          **it gets dark later**

# Contents pages, glossaries and indexes

A contents page helps us find the part or section of the book that we want. It saves us flicking through the book, because it tells us the page number of the information we want to read.

**Transport**

Contents

| | |
|---|---|
| The history of transport | Page 2 |
| Trains | Page 4 |
| Buses | Page 6 |
| Aeroplanes | Page 8 |
| Ships | Page 10 |
| Underground | Page 12 |
| Trams | Page 14 |
| Glossary | Page 16 |
| Index | Page 18 |

## Warm up

1. What is the name of the book that the contents page is for? Circle **one** answer.

   **Trams**  **Aeroplanes**  **Buses**  **Transport**

2. On which page would you find a glossary? _____

3. What type of transport would you read about on page 6?

   _____

4. On which page would you read about transport from a long time ago? _____

## Rainforests
### Contents

| | Page no. |
|---|---|
| Introduction | 4 |
| Chapter 1: What is a rainforest? | 6 |
| Chapter 2: Rainforest plants | 8 |
| Chapter 3: Rainforest animals | 10 |
| Chapter 4: Rainforest bugs | 12 |
| Chapter 5: Rainforest people | 14 |
| Chapter 6: Rainforest food | 16 |
| Quiz | 18 |
| Glossary | 20 |
| Index | 22 |

## Test yourself

**5** In which chapter and on which page would you find information about the bugs that are found in the rainforest?

Chapter _____, page _____

**6** What will you read about in Chapter 6? _____

**7** What sort of questions do you think you would find in the quiz on page 18? Tick **one** answer.

- Questions about the glossary. ☐
- Questions about the whole rainforest. ☐
- Questions about the index. ☐

**8** What information will you find on page 8?

_____

## Challenge yourself

**9** Where would you find the meaning of the word rainforest?

_____

### How did you do?

# Instructions

We follow many different kinds of instructions – recipes, game rules, how to make things and how to do things.

## How to Make Cheese on Toast

You will need:
- one slice of bread
- a handful of grated cheese
- a grill
- a plate

1. First, wash your hands.
2. Then, neatly sprinkle the grated cheese on the slice of bread.
3. Next, carefully place the bread and cheese on the grill pan. Ask an adult to turn the grill on.
4. After two minutes, politely ask an adult to turn the grill off, remove the cheese on toast and put it on a plate.
5. Let it cool for a few minutes (hot cheese can burn your mouth!).
6. Finally, eat and enjoy!

**Top Tip!** Add a blob of tomato sauce to dip your cheese on toast in. Yummy!

## Warm up

1. What does the recipe instruct you to make?
   _____

2. How much grated cheese do you need to make your cheese on toast? Circle **one** answer.

   **a mouthful**  **a spoonful**  **a handful**  **a cupful**

3. What should you do before you start to make your cheese on toast? Circle **one** answer.

   **watch TV**  **brush your hair**  **wash your hands**

## Test yourself

4. What is the last thing the recipe instructs you to do?

   _____ and _____

## Challenge yourself

5. Why do you think you should ask an adult to remove the cheese on toast from the grill and put it on a plate? Circle **one** answer.

   **because it will be hot**   **in case you drop it**   **in case it's sticky**

6. What might happen to the cheese on toast if you didn't turn off the grill after two minutes?

   _____

7. Read the Top Tip again. Tick **one** word that means the same as 'yummy'.
   - sloppy ☐
   - horrible ☐
   - tasty ☐
   - chewy ☐

## How did you do?

# Progress test 1

**Autumn**

In autumn, leaves turn brown and fall off the trees. We dig up the vegetables that were planted in spring. Temperatures start to drop, and there might be frost. Some animals, such as mice and squirrels, prepare for winter by gathering nuts to store in their nests.

## Progress test 1

**1** Who is digging? _____

**2** What is Dad doing? Tick **one** answer.

Dad is sniffing at the potatoes in the basket. ☐

Dad is putting carrots in the basket. ☐

Dad is putting potatoes in the basket. ☐

**3** Find and circle the sign for the **onions**.

**4** What colour is the **cat**? _____

**5** Find and circle the rake.

**6** What do you think the rake is for? Circle **one** answer.

**digging up the vegetables**     **clearing up the fallen leaves**

**to stop the shed falling over**

**7** Name **two** things that happen to the leaves in autumn.

_____ and _____

**8** In which season do we plant vegetables? _____

**9** What happens to the temperatures in autumn?

_____

**10** How do squirrels prepare for winter? Circle **one** answer.

**by eating potatoes**     **by digging up vegetables**

**by gathering nuts**

# Book covers

You can tell so much about what a book is about from its front cover. Sometimes it's the picture on the cover that makes you want to read it.

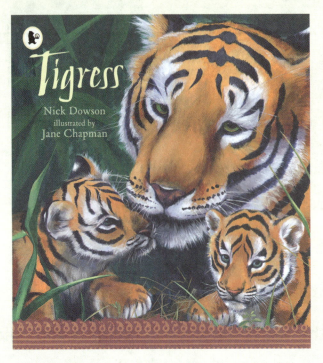

Illustrations © 2004 Jane Chapman. From TIGRESS by Nick Dowson & Illustrated by Jane Chapman. Reproduced by permission of Walker Books Ltd, London, www.walker.co.uk

## Warm up

**1** What is the title of the book? _____

**2** Who wrote the book? _____

**3** What do you think a tigress is? Circle **one** answer.

    **a male tiger**        **a female tiger**        **a baby tiger**

You can find more information about a book by reading the back cover.

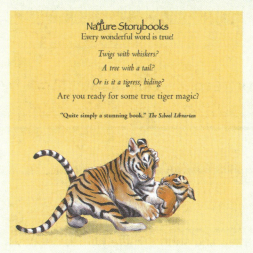

Illustrations © 2004 Jane Chapman. From TIGRESS by Nick Dowson & Illustrated by Jane Chapman. Reproduced by permission of Walker Books Ltd, London, www.walker.co.uk

## Test yourself

**4** How has the book been described by *The School Librarian*? Circle **one** word.

**simple**         **magic**         **stunning**         **wonderful**

**5** Do you think the cubs in the picture are playing or fighting? Give a reason for your answer.

_____

## Challenge yourself

**6** Is the book fiction or non-fiction, and how do you know? Tick **one**.

  fiction, because it's a made-up story ☐
  non-fiction, because it says it's true ☐
  fiction, because it's about a tigress ☐

**7** Who is the question 'Are you ready for some true tiger magic?' aimed at? Circle **one** answer.

**the tigress**         **the school librarian**         **the reader**

How did you do?

# Stories 1

**From *Percy the Park Keeper – One Snowy Night* by Nick Butterworth**

One winter's night it was so cold it began to snow. Great big snowflakes fell past the window of Percy's hut.

"Brr," said Percy. "I think I'll need an extra blanket tonight."

He made himself some hot cocoa and got ready for bed.

Suddenly, Percy heard a tapping sound. There was somebody at the door.

"Now who can that be at this time of night?" thought Percy. He went to the door and looked out.

There on the step was a squirrel. It looked very cold and miserable.

"I can't get to sleep, Percy," said the squirrel. "My bed is full of snow."

"Oh dear," said Percy. "Never mind, I've got plenty of room for two."

The squirrel snuggled down next to Percy and soon began to feel warm.

Knock! Knock! It was the door again.

"Now who can that be?" thought Percy.

Standing outside were two shivering rabbits.

"It's f-freezing," said one rabbit.

"We're f-frozen," said the other.

"You poor things," said Percy. "Come in and warm up."

The rabbits squeezed into the bed next to Percy and the squirrel. There wasn't much room.

"Could you face the other way?" Percy asked the squirrel. "Your tail is tickling my nose."

Knock! Knock!

"Oh dear," said Percy. "Now there's someone else at the door!"

## Warm up

**1** Where does Percy live? Circle **one** answer.

   in a house     in a cottage     in a caravan     in a hut

**2** What sound does Percy make that tells you he is cold?

_____

## Test yourself

**3** Why do you think Percy says he'll need an extra blanket?

_____

**4** When Percy hears the tapping sound, does he know who is at the door? Give a reason for your answer.

_____

**5** Which two words does the writer use to describe how the squirrel looked?

_____ and _____

**6** Why can't the squirrel get to sleep?

_____

## Challenge yourself

**7** Write a sentence about what Percy did that shows he is a kind person.

_____

_____

## How did you do?

# Play scripts

**Sally's Sore Knee**

**Sally:** OUCH! I've hurt my knee!
**Mum:** Sit down and I'll look at it.
**Sally:** It really hurts. Be careful, it's stinging.
**Mum:** How did you do it?
**Sally:** I was jumping off the wall and I fell.
**Mum:** Well, that was a bit silly, Sally, wasn't it?
**Sally:** I know, but everyone else was doing it.
**Mum:** Yes, but everyone else didn't fall. And I've told you before about jumping off that wall. Promise you won't do it again.
**Sally:** I won't.

### Warm up

1. What sound does Sally make that tells you she's in pain? _____

2. What does Mum tell Sally to do? _____

3. How did Sally hurt her knee?
   _____

### Test yourself

4. What reason does Sally give for jumping off the wall?
   _____

5. What do you think Mum might have put on Sally's knee to help make it better?
   _____

# Answers

**Pages 4–5 'Symbols, signs and labels'**
1.

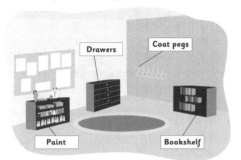

2. a) airport b) toilets c) farm
3. Birdbath
4. Hutch
5. Bench

**Pages 6–7 'Posters'**
1. Honley Hall
2. 8th March
3. 6pm
4. a concert
5. £4
6. three days
7. £6
8. exclamation mark
9. clowns

**Pages 8–9 'Adverts'**
1. Doctor Spock Space Boots come in all sizes. Doctor Spock Space Boots come in all colours.
2. winter
3. 20 years
4. children
5. Answers will vary
6. £5

**Pages 10–11 'Information texts'**
1. cutting the grass
2. planting seeds
3. a ball
4. buds
5. pink
6. The <u>dog</u> is chasing the <u>cat</u>.
7. cake
8. not enough water
9. it gets dark later

**Pages 12–13 'Contents pages, glossaries and indexes'**
1. Transport
2. page 16
3. Buses
4. page 2
5. Chapter 4, page 12
6. Rainforest food
7. Questions about the whole rainforest.
8. Information about rainforest plants
9. In the glossary

**Pages 14–15 'Instructions'**
1. cheese on toast
2. a handful
3. wash your hands
4. Eat and enjoy!
5. because it will be hot
6. It might burn.
7. tasty

**Pages 16–17 'Progress test 1'**
1. Mum
2. Dad is putting potatoes in the basket.
3. Check pupils have circled the sign for the onions in the picture.
4. black and white/grey
5. Check pupils have circled the rake in the picture.
6. clearing up the fallen leaves
7. they turn brown and they fall off the trees
8. spring
9. They start to drop.
10. by gathering nuts

**Pages 18–19 'Book covers'**
1. *Tigress*
2. Nick Dowson
3. a female tiger
4. stunning
5. Answers will vary.
6. non-fiction, because it says it's true
7. the reader

**Pages 20–21 'Stories 1'**
1. in a hut
2. Brr

# Answers

3. Because he's cold. / To keep him warm.
4. No, because he thinks, "Now who can that be (at this time of night)?"
5. cold and miserable
6. Because his bed is full of snow.
7. Percy lets the squirrel and the rabbits come into his hut/bed so they can get warm.

**Pages 22–23 'Play scripts'**
1. OUCH!
2. sit down
3. She jumped off the wall and she fell.
4. Everyone else was doing it.
5. a plaster/a bandage
6. Martin
7. She's surprised/shocked/frightened.
8. a teacher/PE teacher/head teacher
9. because it's Sports Day

**Pages 24–25 'Stories 2'**
1. Fiona and Mum
2. a squeaky toy and a teddy bear
3. cuddly and soft
4. Mrs Harper
5. Any **two** of the following: little, sleepy, beautiful, shiny, black
6. She thought it would be smooth.
7. She loved him.

**Pages 26–27 'Progress test 2'**
1. going on holiday
2. suitcase/roofbox on the roof / the title is 'Family holiday'
3. four
4. suitcase
5. on a boat/ferry/ship
6. Answers will vary. For example, excited, happy, seasick.
7. Check pupils have written appropriate sentences.
8. Check pupils' pictures and sentences.

**Pages 28–29 'Poetry 1'**
1. 24 (four and twenty)
2. The birds began to sing.

3. the king — in the parlour
   the queen — in the garden
   the maid — in the counting house
4. Put those monkeys straight to bed!
5. Because the monkeys banged their heads.
6. There were <u>three</u> boys. There were <u>two</u> girls.

**Pages 30–31 'Poetry 2'**
1. Daddy fell into the pond.
2. a camera
3. the camera
4. he crawled
5. They quacked.
6. a male duck
7. silly

**Pages 32–33 'Traditional tales 1'**
1. in an old, rickety house
2. Because they were poor.
3. sell her at the market
4. beans
5. She screamed. She threw the beans out of the window.
6. There was a giant beanstalk. / A giant beanstalk had grown.
7. They were loud/big/made by someone big.
8. Because Jack chopped the beanstalk down.

**Pages 34–35 'Traditional tales 2'**
1. Hansel and Gretel
2. their father and step-mother
3. nasty
4. sweets, cakes, biscuits, cream, ice-cream, chocolate and jam
5. biscuit
6. they are bony/skinny/thin
7. Their step-mother had gone/wasn't there.

**Pages 36–37 'Traditional tales 3'**
1. how fast he could run
2. all the animals (in the forest)
3. the cheering animals
4. speedy
5. not once

# Answers

6. because the tortoise was so slow
7. Answers will vary. Accept references to 'don't show off', 'slow can be good', 'fast isn't always best'.

## Pages 38–39 'Traditional tales 4'
1. a mouse
2. the king's hunters
3. repay his kindness
4. came to help the lion
5. chewed
6. Because she was so small.
7. Because she freed him/saved him.

## Pages 40–41 'Progress test 3'
1. His eye is falling off.
2. sew her ears back on
3. very silly
4. last summer
5. she still loved him / just the same / she didn't think he looked silly
6. Answers will vary. Example: She doesn't agree because she says 'Hmmm' which sounds like she thinks it isn't different.
7. The wheel has fallen off.
8. She offers to glue the wheel back on.
9. Answers will vary. Example: No, because it's not their fault. No, because he should still love them the same. No, because he should have taken more care of them. Yes, because I think my toys look silly when they are broken. (This last answer could lead to an interesting group discussion.)

### Martin the Martian

*Martin the Martian lands on Earth just as Amil and Connie are walking to school.*

**Amil:** Where do you come from?
**Martin:** Mars. It's a long, long way from here. I landed my space ship in that big field over there. My name's Martin.
**Connie:** My goodness! You're a Martian? So that's why you have green skin, four hands and huge, webbed feet! Not to mention the extra eye on the back of your head. I'm Connie and this is Amil.
**Amil:** Never mind that – you've landed in our school field! And it's Sports Day today!
**Martin:** What's Sports Day? We don't have that on Mars.
**Amil:** Mr Brooks will go mad! We have to set up the field after registration.
**Martin:** Don't worry – whatever 'set up' means, I'll help you.
**Connie:** Thanks, Martin. Sometimes an extra pair of hands comes in very useful.

## Challenge yourself

**6** Who speaks this line? *Don't worry – whatever 'set up' means, I'll help you.* _____

**7** Why do you think Connie says, *My goodness!* when she realises Martin is a Martian? _____

**8** Who might Mr Brooks be? _____

**9** Why do the children need to set up the field after registration?

### How did you do?

# Stories 2

**Fiona's New Puppy**

Fiona was excited. Today she and Mum were going to the farm to collect their new puppy. Fiona had already put a cuddly, soft blanket in a basket and used her birthday money to buy a squeaky toy and a teddy bear for him.

At the farm, Mrs Harper, the farmer, took Fiona and Mum into the barn. There in the corner, snuggled into the straw and fast asleep, was their little puppy!

"Wow!" whispered Fiona. "He's the most beautiful puppy I've ever seen!" Slowly, the sleepy puppy opened his eyes. His nose twitched and he scrambled to his feet. He looked like a ball of shiny, black fur! Fiona put out her hand, and he gently licked it with his tiny, pink tongue.

"It feels funny," said Fiona. "I thought it would be smooth, but it's rough."

Mrs Harper bent down and scooped the puppy up into her arms. "Here," she said to Fiona, "you can hold him."

Nervously, Fiona held out her arms. The puppy snuffled and snuggled against her chest. He felt silky and soft. Fiona felt she would never be able to let him go.

Fiona and her mum and the puppy got in the car.

"Look after him," said Mrs Harper as she waved goodbye.

"We will," replied Fiona.

"What shall we call him?" asked Mum.

"Snuffles!" said Fiona.

## Warm up

**1** Who went to the farm to collect the new puppy? Circle **one** answer.

    **Mum and Dad**        **Fiona and Mum**        **Fiona and Dad**

**2** Name **two** things that Fiona bought with her birthday money.

_____ and _____

**3** Which **two** words are used to describe the blanket that Fiona put in the basket?

_____ and _____

## Test yourself

**4** What was the farmer's name? _____

**5** Write **two** words that describe what the puppy looks like.

_____ and _____

## Challenge yourself

**6** Why was Fiona surprised that the puppy's tongue was rough?

_____

**7** The writer says: *Fiona felt she would never be able to let him go.* What does this tell you about Fiona's feelings for the puppy? Tick **one** box.

    She didn't want the farmer to have him. ☐
    She loved him. ☐
    She was worried he would run away. ☐
    She didn't want him. ☐

## How did you do?

# Progress test 2

**Family holiday**

1.

2.

3.

4.

# Progress test 2

**1** What do you think the family is doing in the first picture? Tick **one** box.

   going to the shops ☐
   going to school ☐
   going on holiday ☐

**2** What is the clue that makes you think that?

_____

**3** How many people are in the car? _____

**4** Look at the first picture. Can you spot something that the family have forgotten?

_____

**5** Look at the last picture. Where is the family now?

_____

**6** How do you think the family might be feeling as they travel on the boat?

_____

**7** Write a sentence beside each picture on page 28 to describe what is happening.

**8** Draw a fifth picture showing the family on the first day of their holiday. Write a sentence below describing what they are doing.

# Poetry 1

**Sing a Song of Sixpence**

Sing a song of sixpence, a pocket full of rye,
Four and twenty blackbirds baked in a pie.
When the pie was opened the birds began to sing,
Oh wasn't that a dainty dish to set before the king?

The king was in his counting house counting out his money,
The queen was in the parlour eating bread and honey,
The maid was in the garden hanging out the clothes,
When down came a blackbird and pecked off her nose!

## Warm up

1. How many blackbirds were baked in the pie? _____

2. What happened when the pie was opened?
   _____

3. Draw a line to match up the people on the left with the places they can be found on the right.

   the king                in the garden
   the queen               in the counting house
   the maid                in the parlour

### Five Little Monkeys

Five little monkeys jumping on the bed,
One fell off and bumped his head.
Mother called the doctor and
the doctor said,
"No more monkeys jumping on
the bed!"

Four little monkeys jumping on
the bed,
One fell off and bumped her head.
Mother called the doctor and
the doctor said,
"No more monkeys jumping on
the bed!"

Three little monkeys jumping on
the bed,
One fell off and bumped his head.
Mother called the doctor and
the doctor said,
"No more monkeys jumping on
the bed!"

Two little monkeys jumping on
the bed,
One fell off and bumped her head.
Mother called the doctor and the
doctor said,
"No more monkeys jumping on
the bed!"

One little monkey jumping on
the bed,
He fell off and bumped his head.
Mother called the doctor and the
doctor said,
"Put those monkeys straight to bed!"

## Test yourself

**4** What did the doctor say when the last little monkey fell off the bed and bumped his head?

_____

## Challenge yourself

**5** Why do you think Mother called the doctor?

_____

**6** How many monkeys were boys and how many were girls?
There were _____ boys.
There were _____ girls.

### How did you do?

# Poetry 2

**When Daddy Fell into the Pond** by Alfred Noyes

Everyone grumbled. The sky was grey.
We had nothing to do and nothing to say.
We were nearing the end of a dismal day,
And there seemed to be nothing beyond,
THEN
Daddy fell into the pond!

And everyone's face grew merry and bright,
And Timothy danced for sheer delight.
"Give me the camera, quick, oh quick!
He's crawling out of the duckweed."
Click!

Then the gardener suddenly slapped his knee,
And doubled up, shaking silently,
And the ducks all quacked as if they were daft
And it sounded as if the old drake laughed.
O, there wasn't a thing that didn't respond
WHEN
Daddy fell into the pond!

## Warm up

1. What happened in the first verse of the poem? Tick **one** answer.

   Mummy fell into the pond. ☐

   Daddy fell into the pond. ☐

   Timothy fell into the pond. ☐

2. What did Timothy ask for in the second verse of the poem? Circle **one** answer.

   a dance     a fishing rod     a camera     some duckweed

## Test yourself

3. What do you think made the 'Click!' sound in the second verse of the poem?

   _____

4. How did Daddy come out of the duckweed? Circle **one** answer.

   he scurried          he hopped          he crawled

5. What did the ducks do when Daddy fell into the pond?

   _____

## Challenge yourself

6. What do you think a 'drake' is? Circle **one** answer.

   a male duck          a large swan          a tiny fish

7. Circle the word below that has a similar meaning to 'daft'.

   silly          cold          kind          sorry

### How did you do?

# Traditional tales 1

**Jack and the Beanstalk**

Once upon a time, a boy called Jack and his mum lived in an old, rickety house. They were so poor that they were cold and hungry all the time. Jack's mum said, "Take our cow to the market and sell her. Make sure you get a good price."

Jack took the cow to the market but he could only sell her for beans! Big, brown beans! When Jack's mum saw the beans, she was very cross. "Beans?" she screamed. "We can't live on a handful of *beans*!" And she threw the beans out of the window.

Imagine their surprise the next day when the beans had grown into a gigantic beanstalk! Jack decided to climb up it. He climbed and he climbed and he climbed. At the top of the beanstalk there was a HUGE castle. Slowly, Jack crept through the enormous, creaky door. On the table was a hen who was laying golden eggs! Jack couldn't believe his eyes! As he grabbed the hen and the golden eggs, he heard heavy footsteps. It was the massive giant who lived in the castle.

"FEE FI FO FUM! I'm coming to get you, so you'd better RUN!"

Jack ran and he ran and he ran, then he scrambled back down the beanstalk, carrying the hen and the golden eggs.

"FEE FI FO FUM! I'm coming to get you, so you'd better RUN!"

The giant was coming after him! At the bottom of the beanstalk, Jack got an axe and he chopped and he chopped and he chopped. The beanstalk fell down and the giant tumbled to the ground. And that was the end of him.

Jack and his mum used the golden eggs to buy food and clothes, and they lived happily ever after.

### Warm up

1. Where did Jack and his mum live? Circle **one** answer.

   **at the top of a beanstalk**    **in an old, rickety house**

   **in a huge castle**

2. Why were Jack and his mum cold and hungry?

   _____

3. What did Jack's mum tell him to do with the cow? Circle **one** answer.

   **take her to the field**   **give her to the giant**   **sell her at the market**

### Test yourself

4. What did Jack get paid for the cow at the market? _____

5. What **two** things did Jack's mum do that showed she was cross?

   _____

6. Why were Jack and his mum surprised the next day?

   _____

### Challenge yourself

7. Jack heard 'heavy footsteps'. What does the word 'heavy' tell you about the footsteps?

   _____

8. Why did the giant tumble to the ground?

   _____

### How did you do?

# Traditional tales 2

**Hansel and Gretel**

Once upon a time, deep in the forest, lived a little boy and a little girl called Hansel and Gretel. They lived in a cottage with their father and their step-mother.

Now, their step-mother wasn't very nice. They were very poor, and there wasn't a lot of money to buy food, so their step-mother was always nagging at their father, saying, "Those children eat too much food! You need to get rid of them!" Can you imagine how frightened the children were?

So one day, when Hansel and Gretel's father had been nagged and nagged, he took them deeper and deeper into the forest and left them there. Can you imagine how terrified the children were?

Hansel and Gretel held hands and walked for hours and hours. At last, they came across a cottage. Now this was no ordinary cottage, for it was made of sweets and cakes and biscuits and cream and ice-cream and chocolate and jam! Can you imagine how excited the children were?

After eating a chocolate door handle, Hansel and Gretel knocked on the biscuity door. A croaky voice said, "Come in, come in!" The children walked in and found an old woman with a pointy nose. "My goodness, what bony birds you are! You won't take long to cook." Can you imagine how scared the children were?

The old woman threw Hansel into a cage and bent down to light the oven. Gretel lifted her foot and SHOVED the old woman's bottom with all her strength! The old woman flew into the oven and that was the end of her! Can you imagine how pleased the children were?

Before they left the cottage, they found a chocolate egg full of golden coins which they put in their pockets. In the forest, they found their father.

"Thank goodness I've found you! Your wicked step-mother has gone. Let's go home." Can you imagine how happy the children were?

So home they went, and they lived happily ever after.

## Warm up

1. What are the names of the children in the story? Circle **one** answer.

   **Hansel and Gretel**     **Gretsel and Hantel**

   **Grensel and Hartel**

2. Who did the children live with? Circle **one** answer.

   **their mother and father**     **their father and step-mother**

   **their mother and step-father**

3. Which word below best describes the children's step-mother? Circle **one** answer.

   **kind**     **nasty**     **happy**     **sad**

## Test yourself

4. Name **seven** things that the old woman's cottage was made of.

   _____

   _____

5. Which word is used to describe the door of the old woman's cottage?

   _____

## Challenge yourself

6. Why does the old woman think the children won't take long to cook?

   _____

7. Why do you think it was safe for the children to go home?

   _____

## How did you do?

# Traditional tales 3

**The Hare and the Tortoise**

There was once a very speedy hare who showed off about how fast he could run. A tortoise, who was fed up with hearing the hare boasting and bragging, challenged him to a race. All the animals in the forest gathered to watch.

The hare ran down the road as fast as he could, then paused to look back at the tortoise. He cried out, "How do you think you're going to win this race when you're so, so slow?" Then he sped off.

The tortoise didn't reply. He just carried on plodding down the road.

The hare flopped down on a grassy hillock beside the road and dozed off. "There's plenty of time for me to relax," he said to himself.

The tortoise walked and walked. He strolled past the hare, who didn't wake up. On and on the tortoise plodded and plodded. He didn't stop – not once – until he came to the finish line.

The animals who were watching cheered so loudly for the tortoise that they woke up the hare.

The hare stretched and yawned and began to run again – but it was too late! The tortoise had crossed the line.

"Slow and steady wins the race," said the tortoise.

After that, the hare never boasted about his speed again.

## Warm up

1) What did the hare show off about? Circle **one** answer.

**how fast he could run**   **how much he could eat**

**how handsome he was**

2) Who watched the hare and the tortoise race?

_____

3) What woke the hare up? Circle **one** answer.

**his alarm clock**   **a thunderstorm**   **the cheering animals**

## Test yourself

4) Which word in the first sentence means the same as 'fast'?

_____

5) How often did the tortoise stop during the race? Circle **one** answer.

**once**     **twice**     **not once**

6) Why did the hare think he had time to relax? Tick **one** answer.

because the race hadn't started ☐

because the tortoise was so slow ☐

because the tortoise had fallen asleep ☐

## Challenge yourself

7) What lesson do you think the hare learned from the tortoise?

_____

**How did you do?**

# Traditional tales 4

### The Lion and the Mouse

An enormous lion lay asleep in the forest, his great head resting on his gigantic front paws. Along came a timid little mouse who ran across the lion's nose. The lion woke with a start and laid his huge paw angrily on the tiny, frightened creature.

"Don't eat me!" begged the mouse. "Please let me go and one day I will repay your kindness."

The lion laughed at the idea of the little mouse being able to help him, but he lifted his paw and let her go.

Some weeks later, the king's hunters caught the lion in a net. While they went to fetch a wagon to carry him, they tied him to a tree.

Just then the mouse scampered by. When she saw the lion, she scurried over to help him. She gnawed and she gnawed at the ropes, and eventually the lion was free. The grateful lion thanked the kind little mouse again and again.

"You were kind to me, and now I have returned the favour. Was I not right? Even a little mouse can help a massive lion!" said the mouse.

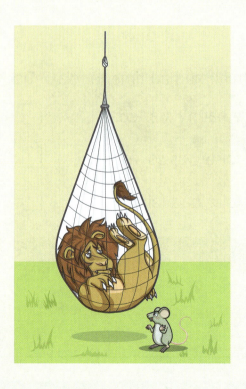

## Warm up

**1** Who woke the lion up from his sleep?

_____

**2** Who caught the lion in their net?

_____

## Test yourself

**3** What did the mouse promise to do if the lion let her go?
Tick **one** answer.

    tell the king about his kindness ☐

    repay his kindness ☐

    never bother him again ☐

**4** What did the little mouse do when she saw the lion tied to a tree?
Circle **one** answer.

**ran to get help**        **went to tell the king**

      **came to help the lion**

**5** Find the sentence: *She gnawed and she gnawed at the ropes* … What does the word 'gnawed' mean? Circle **one** word.

**cut**      **chewed**      **unpicked**

## Challenge yourself

**6** Why did the lion laugh at the idea of the mouse being able to help him?

_____

**7** Why was the lion grateful to the mouse?

_____

## How did you do?

# Progress test 3

### The Jumble Sale

**Mummy:** Sam, have you got any old toys for the jumble sale?

**Sam:** There's Ted, but one of his eyes is falling off. And there's Bunny, but her ears are falling off.

**Mummy:** I can sew them back on and they will be as good as new.

**Sam:** But then I won't want to give them away!

**Mummy:** So, you don't want them when something has gone wrong with them?

**Sam:** Well, they look very silly.

**Mummy:** I didn't think you looked very silly when you broke your arm last summer. I still loved you just the same.

**Sam:** But that's *different*, Mummy!

**Mummy:** Hmmm. Alright, if you don't want to give Ted and Bunny to the jumble sale when they have been mended, what else can you think of?

**Sam:** Well, I've got a car with a wheel that's fallen off.

**Mummy:** I can glue that back on and it will be as good as new.

**Sam:** But then I won't want to give it away!

**Mummy:** Sam, why don't we spend a day fixing all your broken toys? I'll bake some cakes for the jumble sale instead.

# Progress test 3

**1** What is wrong with Ted? Circle **one** answer.

**His ear is falling off.**     **His paw has fallen off.**

**His eye is falling off.**

**2** What does Mummy offer to do to make Bunny as good as new?
_____

**3** Which **two** words does Sam use to describe how Ted and Bunny look?
_____

**4** When did Sam break his arm? _____

**5** How did Mummy feel about Sam when he broke his arm?
_____

**6** Look at these lines:

**Sam:** But that's *different*, Mummy!

**Mummy:** Hmmm.

Do you think Mummy agrees with Sam? Give a reason for your answer.
_____

**7** What is wrong with Sam's car?
_____

**8** How does Mummy offer to fix the car?
_____

**9** Do you think Sam is right to say that Ted and Bunny look very silly because they are broken? Give a reason for your answer.
_____

41

# Notes page

# Notes page

# Acknowledgements

Published by Keen Kite Books
An imprint of HarperCollins*Publishers* Ltd
The News Building
1 London Bridge Street
London SE1 9GF

ISBN 9780008244590

First published in 2017

10 9 8 7 6 5 4 3 2 1

Text and design © 2017 Keen Kite Books, an imprint of HarperCollins*Publishers* Ltd

Author: Shelley Welsh

The author asserts her moral right to be identified as the author of this work.

All rights reserved. No part of this publication may be reproduced, stored in a retrieval system, or transmitted, in any form or by any means, electronic, mechanical, photocopying, recording or otherwise, without the prior permission of Keen Kite Books.

Series Concept and Commissioning: Michelle I'Anson and Shelley Teasdale
Contributor: Rachel Clarke
Project Manager: Fiona Watson
Editor: Caroline Petherick
Cover Design: Anthony Godber
Inside Concept Design: Paul Oates
Text Design and Layout: QBS Learning
Production: Natalia Rebow
A CIP record of this book is available from the British Library.

**Acknowledgements**

*One Snowy Night* by Nick Butterworth. Reprinted by permission of HarperCollins Publishers Ltd, ©1989, Nick Butterworth

*Percy's Bumpy Ride* by Nick Butterworth. Reprinted by permission of HarperCollins Publishers Ltd, ©1999, Nick Butterworth

**Text From TIGRESS by Nick Dowson & Illustrated by Jane Chapman**
Reproduced by permission of Walker Books Ltd, London
http://www.walker.co.uk
Illustrations © 2004 Jane Chapman
**From TIGRESS by Nick Dowson & Illustrated by Jane Chapman**
Reproduced by permission of Walker Books Ltd, London
HYPERLINK "http://www.walker.co.uk" www.walker.co.uk

"When Daddy Fell into the Pond" by Alfred Noyes. Used by permission of the Estate of Alfred Noyes administered by the Society of Authors.

Images are ©Shutterstock.com, ©HarperCollinsPublishers
and ©Rose and Thorn Creative